Monkey See

a story of global proportion

by
Kevin McBeth

This book is dedicated to every wonderful
little monkey that reads it.

In just a few short centuries
They won't find much of you or me,
Since shelf life, realistically,
Cannot endure finality.

But years before, in monkey trees,
Lived sensible communities.
These monkeys lived for basic need
And cared about necessity.

They thrived on monkey harmony,
Survival's creativity,
And living altruistically
Ensured themselves good company.

As time went on, the tendency
Was that these monkeys could not be
Content with mere simplicity.
They wanted, justifiably.

They climbed down from their monkey trees
To purchase land and property.
They swore by one true monkey creed –
Financial opportunity.

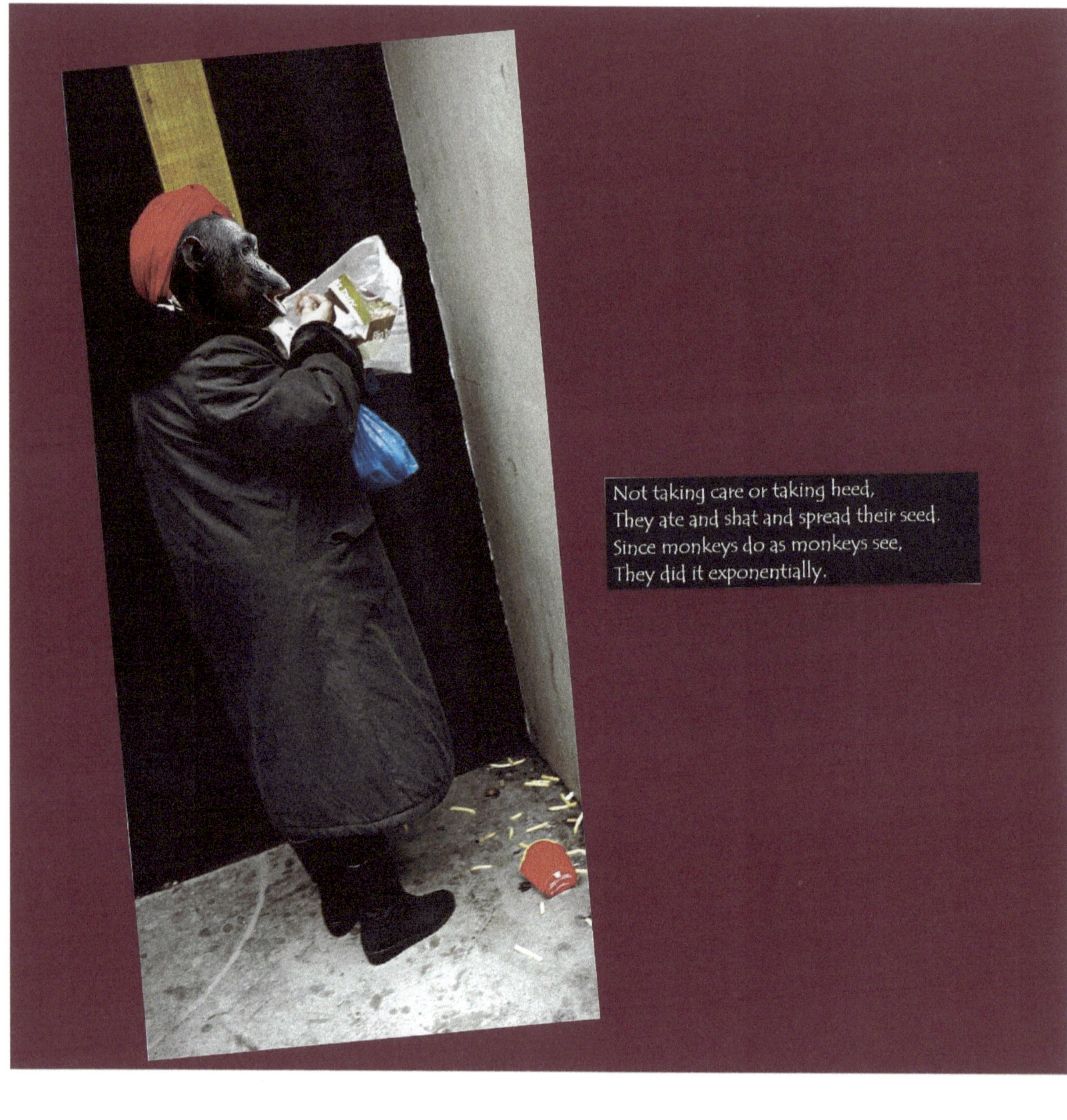

Not taking care or taking heed,
They ate and shat and spread their seed.
Since monkeys do as monkeys see,
They did it exponentially.

They stuffed themselves with monkey greed,
And wined and dined on gluttony.
They fought, destroyed, and killed with glee
Not thinking consequentially.

Their number one activity
Was reproducing casually
So popular, that land and sea
Filled up with popularity.

They built themselves machinery,
And with it, stark dependency.
Each Gigobyte and MP3,
Remote controlled reality.

Through time, their monkey legacy
Of air-conditioned luxury,
Their land of milk and calorie
Evolved to mental atrophy.

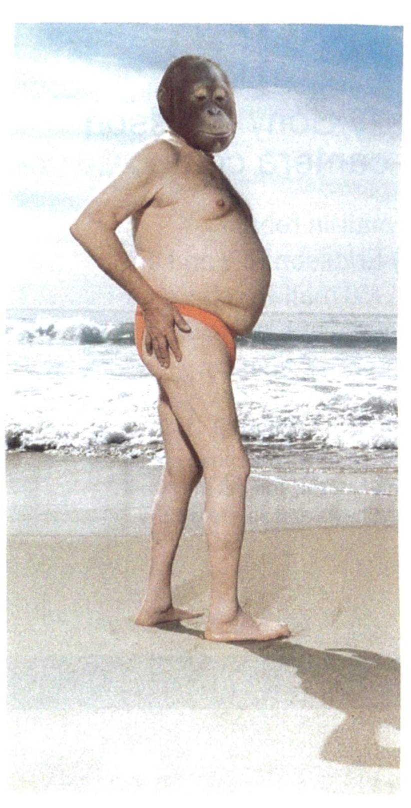

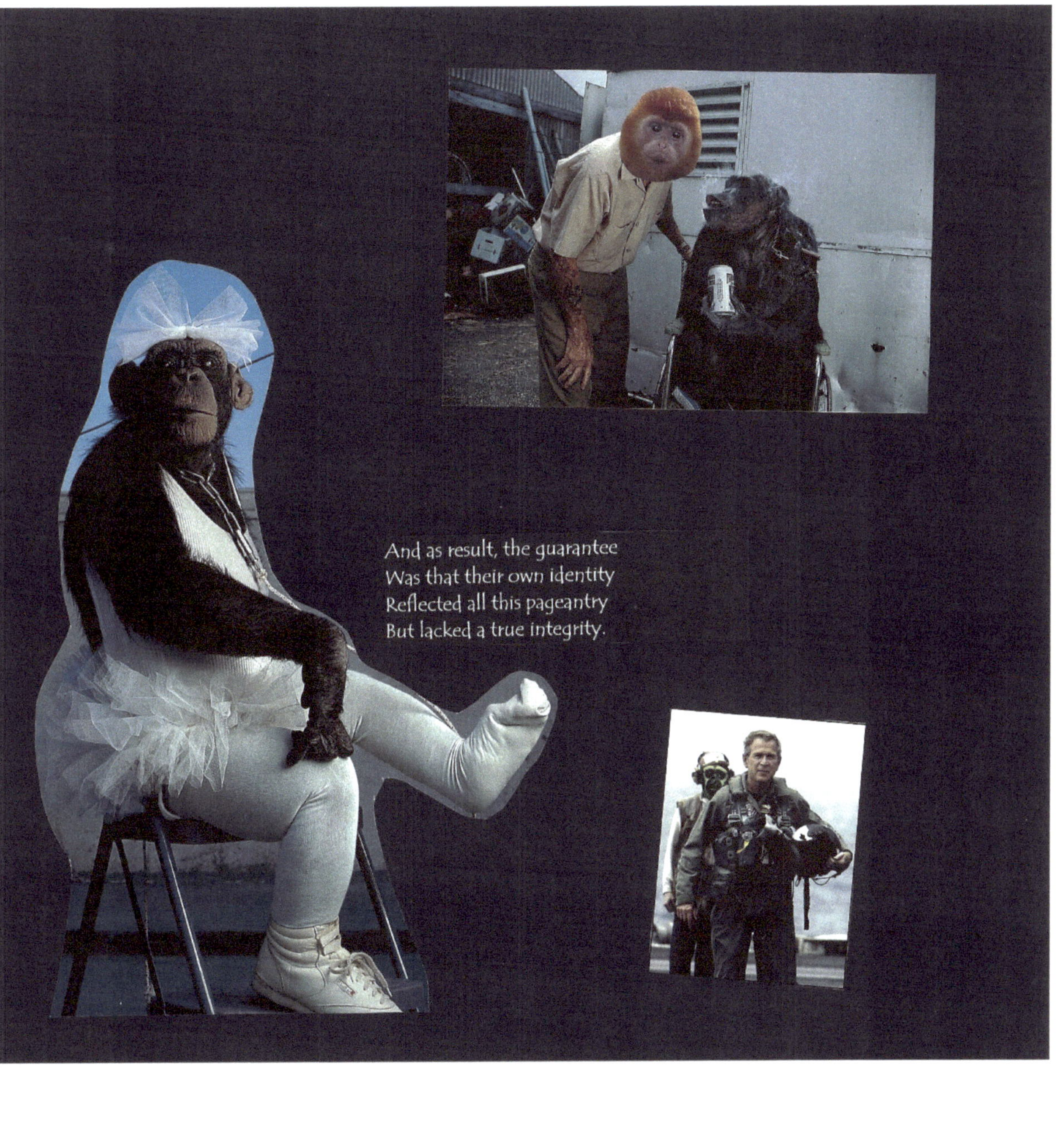

And as result, the guarantee
Was that their own identity
Reflected all this pageantry
But lacked a true integrity.

They watched their vast technology
Define their moral certainty.
But even shiny SUVs
Cannot produce banana trees.

Consuming past capacity,
They made it clear, and all agreed
That even common decency
Is not recycled easily.

And so, the monkeys, rapidly
Ran out of food and air to breathe,
And love and sensitivity –
True monkey life, essentially.

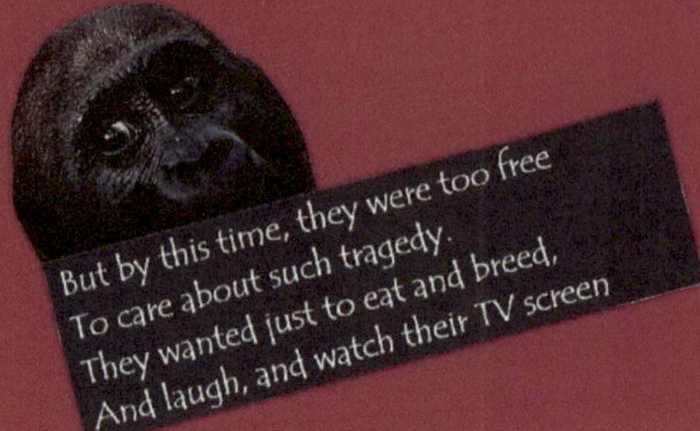
But by this time, they were too free
To care about such tragedy.
They wanted just to eat and breed,
And laugh, and watch their TV screen

W
hap me py

They sat on couches blissfully,
Content with their complacency
Just surfing web and picking flea,
Fast—forwarding their destiny.

And deep within their apathy
Remained the greatest irony –
The gadgets that had made them free
Depended on dependency.

So, in a few short centuries
They won't find much for scrutiny,
Except the monkeys' history
Available on DVD.